Forgiveness
A Two-Way Street

AGLOW CORNERSTONE SERIES

by JoAnne Sekowsky

Women's Aglow Fellowship, Int'l.
P.O. Box I
Lynnwood, WA 98046-1558
USA

Cover design by Beverly Hughes

Unless otherwise noted, all Scripture quotations in this publication are from the Holy Bible, New International Version. Copyright ©1973, 1978, 1984, International Bible Society.

ISBN 0-930756-95-9

Write for a free catalog.

Introduction

H ave you ever been badly in debt? Have you ever owed someone so much money you had absolutely no way of ever repaying it? How did you feel when it came time to settle up?

Let's say, for the sake of discussion, that when that day came, the person to whom you owed the money took pity on you and canceled the entire debt. How do you think you would have felt then? Would you have been willing to cancel the debt of someone else who owed you money?

Let me tell you a story.

A businessman gave a woman several million dollars to invest for him. Over a period of time she made some very bad investments, and finally, when it came time to settle up the account, she had to tell the businessman that she had lost all his money.

Imagine his reaction. He had trusted her with a fortune and now it was all gone. At first he decided to take her to court to see if he could prove that she had mismanaged his money. However, as the woman pleaded with him, he began to feel sorry for her. Finally, he decided to write off his losses and he completely canceled her debt.

Later that same evening, while the woman was out celebrating her narrow escape, she ran into a very poor friend who owed her $10.00.

"Hey," she greeted her friend, "where's the money you owe me?"

"I'm sorry," the friend explained, "but I've been in the hospital and I haven't been able to work. I'll pay you back as soon as I can."

"That's not good enough," the woman said. "You dig up that money right away or I'm going to see my lawyer."

Her friend pleaded, "C'mon, give me more time. I'll pay you back."

But the woman wouldn't listen, and the next day she called a lawyer to take action.

It so happened that the businessman learned what the woman had done, and he became very angry.

He went to her place of business and confronted her. "I showed you mercy when you couldn't repay me," he reminded her. "Couldn't you have done the same thing for this poor woman? Now because you're so lacking in mercy, I'm going to treat you just like you treated her. I'll see you in court!"

Does this story sound familiar? It should. It's a paraphrase of one Jesus told a group of His followers. However, Jesus didn't end His story there. He concluded it with a thought provoking statement. "This is the way God the Father will treat each of you unless you in turn forgive others," He said (Matt. 18:35).

Imagine the impact His final comment made on His listeners. They had thought Jesus was talking about money and, all the time, He'd been talking about forgiveness. What was He saying, anyway?

Through this story, Jesus is speaking not just to His listeners of 2,000 years ago, but to women and men in all times. Though many conditions have changed since Jesus spoke publicly on a Palestinian hillside, the truth He presents in His teaching applies as much to us today as it did to those people so many years ago.

Jesus had some important ideas for us to consider about our relationship with God. Because they're so important, let's list them:

1. Jesus is informing us that God is like the businessman in the story, who, out of mercy, cancels an enormous debt.

2. He is also telling us that we are like the woman in the story, and our sins against God constitute a debt so enormous that if we could translate its value into monetary terms, we would have to value it at millions of dollars.

3. He is saying, too, that in our own power, we can never repay that debt.

4. Next, Jesus is saying that the sins anyone commits against us are worth only an insignificant amount when compared to our debt to God.

5. He is saying, too, that our natural inclination is *not* to forgive others.

6. Finally, He is saying that whenever we refuse to forgive someone, we block the flow of God's forgiveness to us.

Behind Jesus' words lies a dynamic principle of the Kingdom of Heaven: *We must forgive as we have been forgiven.*

Chapter One

The Biggest Debt in the World

Before we go any further, let's stop to consider the nature of this enormous debt to God.

Our debt is two-fold. First, there is the portion caused by our sin against God. The Bible tells us that *all* have sinned and fall short of the glory of God (Rom. 3:23). We often refuse to believe this about ourself, but the scripture in Romans makes no exceptions. *Everyone* is born with a sinful nature and is in rebellion against God. Until we put our trust in Jesus to free us from the control of that sinful nature, we are, in fact, God's enemies (Rom. 5:10).

It is because of this sinful nature that we commit sins. Many people believe that everything would be fine between them and God if they could quit sinning, but even if they could (and they can't), they would still have a sinful nature which is at war with God.

This sinful nature and its consequences showed itself in the very earliest history of mankind. Cain committed the first murder when he killed Abel. Jealous because God had accepted Abel's sacrifice and not his own, he grew angry. Rather than seek forgiveness from God and make the kind of sacrifice God required, Cain enticed his brother out into a field one day and murdered him.

Not too long afterward, we see Cain's descendant, Lamech, boasting of how he had killed a youth who had wounded him; we also see Jacob, with the help of his mother, Rebecca, deceiving Isaac, and, by trickery, receiving both the birthright and the blessing that belonged to the firstborn. We see Joseph's brothers selling him into slavery, family hatreds growing into tribal feuds, and a system developing which demanded the spilling of blood be avenged by the spilling of more blood. And so it has been throughout history. It is no different in our time.

A single section of one day's newspaper recounts the story of a New York police officer being wounded by a sniper, a U.S. customs agent found shot to death, a report of bombing and strafing in Pakistan, a riot in Paris, a woman killed in El Salvador, a boy kidnapped in Iowa—all in the first few pages.

Our world shudders on the brink of a holocaust because of hatred between nations that goes back hundreds, even thousands of years: Arabs against the Jews; Turks against the Armenians; Irish against the Irish and the British; blacks against the whites; the rich against the poor.

If anyone still feels none of this has anything to do with her, consider humanity's corporate guilt.

God gave us a beautiful, perfect world with everything we would ever need; we daily pollute it beyond repair. He gave us the gift of children; we purposely abort them, abuse them and neglect them. He told us to be content with one husband or wife. Successive marriages have been the response of many of us. He admonished us to share. A few countries of the world have accumulated up to 90% of the world's wealth. He gave us the opportunity to make all men our brothers—we have responded with ghettos, restricted housing, and apartheid.

Matthew 21:33-46 recounts the parable of the landowner who sent His servants to collect from the tenants what was due him. First the tenants beat and killed the servants and, when the landowner finally in one last chance sent His son, they killed him, too. This is humanity's story.

Individually, members of the human race have not fared much better. In most people's life anger, envy, bitterness, and unforgiveness spawn an insidious cancer that attacks the fiber and structure of their health and most of their relationships.

Can anyone still doubt the existence of a sin nature in all of us?

Although this sin nature and its consequences make our debt to God enormous, they constitute only half of that debt.

While we were lost in our sins, and had accumulated this enormous debt, we were in a hopeless situation. Because we could never pay it off, we deserved any punishment God might devise for us.

That's when God had compassion on us. Because we were so helpless, He decided to forgive our debt. That got us off the hook, but a problem remained. In God's economy, the debt still existed: someone had to pay it for us. God chose to take the responsibility on Himself, and He sent His Son, Jesus, to pay it. Obediently, Jesus took our punishment (paid our debt) by dying. In this one act

6

of obedience, He broke the power of our sin nature once and for all. God accepted His Son's sacrifice as sufficient payment for our debt. Now, when we accept Jesus as Savior, He marks our account *Paid in Full.*

The only condition God attaches to this transaction is that we keep our account free and clear of charges. Just as we have been forgiven, we in turn must forgive anyone who offends us.

Chapter Two
The $10.00 Debt

W hy do we find forgiveness so difficult? Let's take a look at some life situations and see if we can discover an important clue.

Laura and Jill, best friends since grade school, went away to college together where they shared a room. Both girls were popular at school and led a very active social life, giving second place to their studies. Just before semester finals, one of their friends managed to get hold of the answer sheet for a chemistry exam. She shared it with all her friends, including Laura and Jill.

A short while later, officials began an investigation of the wholesale cheating on campus. Both girls were questioned. Along with several others, Laura confessed to having cheated and was consequently suspended from school. To her surpise and hurt, Jill and the other students who refused to confess managed to escape suspension for lack of evidence.

Laura, who felt betrayed by her friend's lack of honesty, made no attempt to be reinstated in school following her period of suspension. In the years that have passed since then, she has refused all efforts on Jill's part to see her again.

"I don't want to have anything to do with her," she has more than once told mutual friends. "Jill lacks backbone. She should have admitted her cheating and taken her medicine like some of us did. I'll never forgive her."

* * * * * * * * *

Dan tore up the third letter he'd written to his ex-wife that evening. How he hated that woman! And at times like tonight when he got to missing his kids, he had to express it. For a moment he entertained the idea of calling her on the phone, but it was too easy for her to hang up on him.

He paced the apartment restlessly, then sat down abruptly at the table and started another letter. Jennifer had destroyed his life and stolen his children from him. Somehow he'd make her pay.

* * * * * * * * * *

Every time Joyce thinks of her third-grade teacher, Mrs. Crossley, she feels a burning sensation in the pit of her stomach. The old witch! Mrs. Crossley was a woman who had made life miserable for a very sensitive eight-year-old. Uncoordinated and left-handed, Joyce had nevertheless done fine in school until it was time to learn cursive writing. Remembering the pain of those days still gave her occasional nightmares as an adult.

Without fail nearly every class day, Mrs. Crossley singled out Joyce's papers to ridicule in front of the whole class. In that woman's class, Joyce had grown to hate school, a sentiment that had remained with her until she was sixteen and had dropped out of school.

It was all Mrs. Crossley's fault. Although Joyce earned her GED a few years later, she still carried her resentment with her. If it hadn't been for that mean old woman, she'd probably have gone on to college and gotten a decent education.

* * * * * * * * * *

Do any of these people sound familiar? Probably they do. We all know at least one person like them, someone who is caught up in unhappy relationships or situations, who feels she has been or is being victimized, someone who suffers from unforgiveness.

Perhaps we're even that kind of person.

One of the characteristics of human nature is to minimize and quickly forget the wrongs we do to others, while at the same time magnify the way others hurt us.

According to Jesus, we have it all backwards.

In the story He told, He compared the debts of the two people who owed money—the million-dollars-plus debt and the $10.00 debt. Then comes the hard part: Jesus said no matter how badly someone may have injured us, its importance can never be compared to that of the debt God paid for us—anymore than a $10.00 debt can be compared to one of a million dollars.

This is difficult for us to grasp. God can't be serious. When He decided something like that, He obviously wasn't thinking about the kind of hurts we've experienced. We see our injuries in the $1,000,000 class.

However, God is not going to change His mind about our grievances. He has judged them and declares them to be merely

$10.00 debts. He expects us to see them in the same way.

But God can't really mean that. What about the horrendous crimes people commit everyday?

What about the sexual abuse some small children are forced to endure?

What about the daily terror some people live under?

What about wife beating?

What about the way some of our older citizens are being treated by their own families?

What about drunken drivers who run down and kill innocent people?

What about what Hitler did to the Jews? (We think we have God now, especially with that last one.)

In addition, there are the people who do not physically harm us, but injure us mentally and emotionally. There's also rejection, lying, cheating—few people in our modern world escape childhood without some sort of psychological pain. What about the people who suffer this way?

None of our arguments, however, change God's evaluation of the situation. Compared to our own sinful nature, compared to what Jesus did for us on the cross, the "sins" committed against us are still the less—the $10.00 debt.

If we are ever to be healthy, if we are ever to be whole, if we are ever to be able to forgive, we must accept God's evaluation of our condition and agree with Him.

Chapter Three

Forgiveness—The Key to Wholeness

"*L*ove *your enemies, do good to those who hate you, bless those who curse you, pray for those who mistreat you. If someone strikes you on one cheek, turn to him the other also. If someone takes your cloak, do not stop him from taking your tunic. Give to everyone who asks you and if anyone takes what belongs to you, do not demand it back. Do to others as you would have them do to you*" *(Luke 6:27-31).*

Why does God consider forgiveness so important? Why has He made it one of the foundational principles of His kingdom?

God's desire for His people has always been, will always be, wholeness—physical, mental, and spiritual. Not only has He built into our nature a need to receive forgiveness, but He has also placed in us a need to forgive others. Anger, resentment, bitterness, and unforgiveness—all the negative emotions and attitudes that plague our life—contribute to a host of illnesses, both physical and emotional.

Although doctors are not in total agreement about the role unforgiveness plays in specific illnesses, many agree that it is frequently an ingredient in many major illnesses.

"For centuries scoffers have ridiculed the advice of Jesus, 'Love your enemies,' as impractical, idealistic and absurd. Now psychologists are recommending it as a panacea for many of man's ills," writes Dr. S.I. McMillen, in his modern classic, *None of These Diseases**

---

*Dr. S.I. McMillen, *None of These Diseases* (Fleming H. Revell Co.)

"When Jesus said, *'Forgive seventy times seven', (Matt. 18:22)* He was thinking not only of our souls, but of saving our bodies from ulcerative colitis, toxic goiters, high blood pressure, and scores of other diseases."

Barbara's hypertension became a serious problem after her husband, Bill, wasn't made foreman at the plywood factory where he had worked since he was a young man. "Bill really deserved the job," she complains to any friend who will listen. "It isn't fair—they don't appreciate loyalty anymore. Poor Bill—*I'll never forgive them* for not giving him that job."

The constant rehashing of this same theme bores her friends, and is undoubtedly a major ingredient in her high blood pressure.

Contrast her story with that of Vivian's. Vivian's arthritis began with some early morning stiffness, which rapidly progressed to the point where it was curtailing many of her activities. In prayer one day, the Lord impressed upon her the necessity of forgiving a sister-in-law who had recently been very critical of her. Vivian was obedient, and then forgot about the whole episode. It wasn't until her husband commented one day, several months later, that she no longer walked stiffly that Vivian realized that her arthritis was gone.

Many doctors today admit they are helpless to effectively treat diseases caused or intensified by unforgiveness and anger unless there is a radical change in the patient's emotional outlook. They are unable to cure ailments while the underlying cause remains.

Middle-aged Florence has a recurring ulcer. A friend pointed out that Florence's attacks concided with visits from either of her two older sisters.

While still a little reluctant to admit such a simple explanation for her ulcer attacks, Florence does recognize that each visit causes her to remember unhappy childhood days. The two older sisters, born less than a year apart, had always been close friends as children, a friendship that left little room for baby sister Florence, who desperately wanted to be included.

Today, visits by either sister are usually accompanied by a flood of memories from her childhood days and a flare-up of her ulcer.

What unforgiveness does to our body, however, hardly compares to what it does to our soul. We need only to look around us for examples.

There are people like Lee, who has ruined any chance for a restoration of her marriage by her refusal to forgive her husband, Terry's, one "indiscretion" which happened five years ago.

Although the couple continue to live together, Terry's infidelity absorbs much of Lee's thinking. If Terry says he has to work late, the turmoil is there as strong as ever. If he goes someplace without her, she wonders if he is with another woman. Accusations follow, and Terry has reached the place where the sorrow he felt originally is for the most part gone.

What could have been a restored marriage, quite possibly made stronger than before, has turned into a battlefield of misery and torment for both of them.

Tim is missing the companionship of his three lively grandchildren, all because nine years ago he told his daughter, Louise, he would never forgive her if she married Stan. Louise married Stan anyway and, although she has made several attempts to be reconciled to her father, he has refused to accept them.

Laura has denied herself a warm friendship with her neighbor, Judy, because of her continuing resentment over several incidents that happened between their two children many years ago when both children were in grade school.

The children, who are now in high school, put their differences to rest many years ago, and Judy doesn't even remember the problems. It is only Laura who continues to nourish her "grievances."

Many patients in mental hospitals today are evidence of the devastating contribution lack of forgiveness makes to mental illness. Far too many beds in our nursing and retirement homes are occupied by bitter, unforgiving men and women whose minds have virtually solidified around real and imagined grievances.

An older friend, who felt my pastor should have done more at the time of my mother's last illness and subsequent death, called to let me know how she felt. When I told her that I didn't feel that way, she commented: "Oh, you're too forgiving."

Can anyone be too forgiving? Today this unfortunate lady is spending her final years in a mental hospital.

Frequently, lack of forgiveness erupts into retaliation and revenge. Sometime ago, newspapers chronicled the story of "respectable" Leo Held, who one morning drove to the mill where he worked, armed with several guns, and proceeded to shoot everyone who got in his way. His reasons: a series of minor grievances against a score of people, which he had allowed to infect his thinking.

The human body, our mind, and emotions were designed to function well only when we forgive. They cannot stand the strain and stress that anger, unforgiveness, and bitterness place on them.

Listen to what Dr. McMillen says: "What a person eats is not as important as the bitter spirit, the hates and the feelings of guilt that eat at him. A dose of baking soda in the stomach will never reach those acids that destroy body, mind and soul...

"Running people down doesn't keep us free from a host of diseases of body and mind. The verbal expressions and animosity toward others call forth certain hormones from the pituitary, adrenal, thyroid and other glands, an excess of which can cause disease in any part of the body. Many diseases can develop when we fatten our grudges by rehearsing them in the presence of others."*

Does God's demand for forgiveness mean that some people are free to hurt anyone, while others, who perhaps through no fault of their own, are always victims? Is there never a day of reckoning for the "offenders"?

No, it doesn't mean that at all. It means only that, for the most part, God has reserved for Himself the exclusive rights to administer both justice and punishment. *"Vengeance is mine" (Deut. 32:35 TLB),* God has declared once and for all. Why? For the simple reason that we cannot be trusted to handle judgment. Only God, the righteous Judge, knows all the facts concerned, all the reasons why, and is therefore in a position to judge fairly. He has relieved us of the responsibility of ever having to bear a grudge or take revenge, and the price of doing so would cost us.

God's desire is for our wholeness, and the longer we linger over the unfortunate things others have or have not done to us, the less whole we become.

*Ibid.

Chapter Four

Contamination

S ickness and lack of wholeness are not the only or the final results of unforgiveness in our life. The Bible warns us that when we refuse to forgive, we are not the only victims; our unforgiveness reaches out far beyond ourself and poisons many others. The writer of Hebrews expresses it this way:

Watch out that no bitterness takes root among you, for as it springs up it causes deep trouble, hurting many in their spiritual lives (Heb. 12:15).

One reason God insists on forgiveness in His kingdom is because bitterness and unforgiveness contaminate.

How can bitterness contaminate?

The Modern Language Bible's translation of the verse from Hebrews gives us an important clue. *"See to it that no one falls short of divine grace; that no one cultivates a root of bitterness."*

Cultivate and *root* are both gardening or agricultural terms. *Cultivate* means to prepare the ground or to specially labor and care for.

Let's try on that definition for size.

"See to it that no one falls short of divine grace; that no one prepares the ground by raising a root of bitterness." Or "See that no one falls short of divine grace; that no one aids the growth of a root of bitterness with special labor and care."

What is significant about the writer using the term *root of bitterness* rather than *plant of bitterness,* or *tree of bitterness?* A gardening book helps us understand why.

1. Some roots grow from ten to thirty feet deep.

This one fact alone explains the long life of some of the bitterness from which our world suffers. Longtime conflicts around the globe, national hatreds, regional prejudices—all have deeply buried roots, some of them hundreds of years old.

2. Some roots serve as reproductive organs.

Two high schools in an eastern city had a long-standing football rivalry. No one remembers the original incident, but each time the two teams played, further incidents erupted. One year students from one school spray-painted obscene words on the front of the rival school; another year, after a game, some spirited fans gave a carload of the second school's students a bad time. Each year the tension between the two schools mounted as old grievances fanned new ones. Students from other schools in the same city decided to get into the act, and fighting and brawling became the aftermath of most games.

Finally, the inevitable happened—a student was killed and several others severely injured in the post game action. When last heard from, city officials were seriously considering eliminating all spectators from the high school sports contests in that area.

An acquaintance of mine has subtly taught her daughters to be bitter. Deserted by her husband, Larry, after a quarrel when they were both very young, she has used every opportunity through the years to remind the girls that their difficult life was because "Daddy didn't love us enough to take care of us."

Several years ago, when a repentant Larry tried to reestablish contact with his family, his daughters refused to see him. At present, neither girl has married, and their relationship with men are troubled and unsatisfying.

3. Some root systems grow out of control.

I once had a lovely, heart-shaped flower bed. Every year it produced a variety of flowers in profusion. Then one year, nothing grew.

My neighbor got to work with his pickax, but was barely able to penetrate the ground for more than a few inches. Investigation revealed that the roots of nearby trees had grown and spread themselves beneath my flower garden, which was now little more than a few inches of topsoil covering an almost impenetrable network of roots.

Nell and Billy recently made the newspaper columns when they were divorced. The reason: They were among the oldest couples ever to have been divorced in that city. First their lawyer, then the counselor he sent them to, then the judge, tried to dissuade them from the action. But each gave up in turn as they heard the elderly couple's recital of wrongdoings on the other one's part. Some of the grievances went back to their courtship days. It was as though each had kept a journal or mentally logged in the event every time one or the other erred. Called "dumping" or "gunnypacking," such a practice is a common element in many divorce cases today. In the case of Nell and Billy, the very reluctant judge eventually granted the divorce when it became apparent that neither side had any desire for a reconciliation.

Their marriage was a lot like my flower bed. The few inches of the "topsoil" of their marriage was completely underlaid with an impenetrable network of roots of bitterness.

4. Some roots are incredibly strong.

In a housing development where I once lived, each yard came equipped with a beautiful weeping willow tree. How I delighted in that tree, at first. My delight became less ecstatic a few years later when the roots of the tree began to break and grow through the patio on the one side and the concrete driveway on the other. I had to make a decision: I could either keep the large-rooted weeping willow or I could keep the rest of the yard, including the section where the house sat. Obviously, the tree had to go.

Many bitternesses are like that willow tree; just a seed or slender shoot when first planted, but given the right growing conditions, they can grow powerful enough to destroy almost anything that stands in their way.

5. Weeds are easiest to pull when their roots are small.

I have a friend, Louise, who has the wonderful ability of never letting small annoyances grow into grievances. We once shared a room at a retreat and although Louise got up at least twenty minutes each morning before I did, I was still able to get ready before she did. One morning I started to tease her.

"C'mon, Louise, you've been beautifying yourself for forty-five minutes now. Give the mirror a rest."

Louise took my ribbing good-naturedly for several minutes, then, when I continued, she came over to where I was standing.

"Be a good friend and don't tease me about how long it takes me to get ready," she said, putting her hands on my shoulders. "I know it's dumb, but I react to it."

For a moment I felt a touch of annoyance. How sensitive can you get! But my annoyance was quickly replaced by admiration for her wisdom. Rather than "suffering in silence" as many of us do Louise was telling me that what I was doing annoyed her.

"I'm sorry," I apologized. "I was insensitive."

She gave me a quick hug and the subject ended there. I was glad that Louise hadn't suffered in silence. Had I unknowingly continued to tease her, she might soon have built a case against my insensitivity.

6. Some roots are edible; some are poisonous.

17

While some roots provide us with delicious food, we would never deliberately eat a poisonous root. How differently we sometimes behave in our spiritual eating. The consequences, however, are much the same.

If we feast on the possible sources of bitterness in our life (refusing to forgive and forget), if we lovingly prepare them with delicious sauces and side dishes, gorging ourself with them (remembering at every possible opportunity each offense committed against us), the day will surely come when we've either been poisoned or we've lost our taste for the better food Jesus has to feed us. In time we may even become so satisfied with bitterness we lose all our hunger and thirst for righteousness itself.

Chapter Five

Remade in Christ's Image

There is an another essential reason why forgiveness is one of the foundation stones upon which the Kingdom is built. God's vision is to populate His Kingdom with sons and daughters who are conformed to the image of Christ (Rom. 8:29).

That job of conforming us to Christ is at the heart of everything the Holy Spirit is doing in our life.

To me there is no more beautiful verse in all the Bible than the words from the first chapter of John: *"And the Word became flesh and dwelt among us"* (1 John 1:14 RSV). Why did God take the form of man and come to live among us? One important reason: To demonstrate to us who God is and what He is really like.

The older I grow the more I become aware that, if we are to change, we need role models. God, in His great wisdom, gave us Christ, that we might be modeled after Him. The Bible provides us with sufficient evidence of what Jesus did in a variety of circumstances, how He responded to injustice, offenses and, eventually, excruciating pain and humiliation in His death on the cross.

It is true that, on occasion, Jesus spoke some harsh words; however, they were always in response to a distorted image of His Father, the misuse of His Father's name, injustices to the defenseless. These kinds of things caused Him to angrily confront the authorities of His time—not personal injustice.

When it came to personal injury, Jesus always returned love for hate—He always forgave.

Should we ever doubt this, we have the record of that one magnificent moment on the cross when time stood still and all eternity listened to Jesus' dying prayer, *"Father, forgive them for they do not know what they are doing"* (Luke 23:34).

Jesus is not our only model. The Bible provides many others who serve as models for forgiving. In the Old Testament, we have the picture of Joseph, who having been sold into slavery by his brothers, became their savior in their time of need. That such forgiveness was unique is shown by the brothers' fears. Even after Joseph had assured them that he bore them no ill will, their own guilty consciences allowed them no rest.

When Jacob their father died, their fears intensified. The Bible tells us, *"They sent word to Joseph, saying, 'Your father left these instructions before he died: "This is what you are to say to Joseph: I ask you to forgive your brothers the sins and the wrongs they committed in treating you so badly. Now please forgive the sins of the servants of the God of your father."'*

"When their message came to him, Joseph wept. His brothers then came and threw themselves down before him. 'We are your slaves,' they said.

"But Joseph said to them, 'Don't be afraid. Am I in the place of God? You intended to harm me, but God intended it for good to accomplish what is now being done, the saving of many lives. So then don't be afraid. I will provide for you and your children. And he reassured them and spoke kindly to them" (Gen. 50:16-21).

We also have a model in Abraham. When his herdsmen and those of his nephew, Lot, warred with each other, Abraham suggested that they split up the land. Lot chose that which lay in the direction of Sodom and Gomorrah. He had reason many times to regret his taking advantage of his uncle's generosity. Only a few years later, he was captured and carried off.

It was Abraham who took his fighting men and went out to rescue the younger man. Abraham, knowing his success or failure was dependent upon the Lord, did not have to resent and carry a grudge for what Lot had previously done.

We also have a model in Stephen, the first Christian martyr, who, as the stones hurled against him, fell to his knees, crying, *"Lord, do not hold this sin against them"* (Acts 7:60).

We see this same attitude of ready forgiveness in the Apostle Paul, who rejected and persecuted by the Jews, could still say, *"I could wish that I myself were cursed and cut off from Christ for the sake of my brothers, those of my own race, the people of Israel"* (Rom. 9:3).

Finally, we are given a model in the familiar story of the Prodigal Son found in Luke 15:11-32. We all love this story of the son, who asked for his share of his inheritance, left his home, and went to a far land. There, he wasted his money on "wine, women and song." Finally, after he had lost everything, including his self-respect, and on the verge of starvation, he came to his senses and decided to return to his father for forgiveness. He even prepared a speech.

As he returned to his home, his father, who had been watching for him every day, saw him from afar and rushed out to meet him. Before he had a chance to give his speech, his father forgave him. As a matter of fact, this loving father, whom we all recognize as a picture of our heavenly Father, probably forgave his son long before. This is the way love acts.

The son at this point would have gladly accepted servanthood, but the loving father restored him to sonship. *"Bring the best robe and put it on him. Put a ring on his finger and sandals on his feet."*

Each of these items is a symbol of authority and position.

By way of contrast, this same story provides, in the person of the older brother, the picture of what unforgiveness does. Bitter, rejecting, and unforgiving, this brother nursed his grievances and refused to join in the festivities the father provided for the returning son.

Listen to his accusations: *"Look! All these years I've been slaving for you and never disobeyed your orders! Yet you never gave me even a young goat so I could celebrate with my friends. But when this son of yours who has squandered your property with prostitutes comes home, you kill the fattened calf for him."*

This is an accurate picture of the bitter, unforgiving person:

Self-righteous:	*"All these years I've been slaving for you."*
Keeps score:	*"I never disobeyed you."*
Critical:	*"You never gave me a young goat so I could celebrate with my friends."*
Sees himself as blameless:	*"This son of yours"* (not my brother)
Nurses anger and un-forgiveness:	Refuses to go to the party
Blinded:	Never realized what was available to him all these years

What a sharp contrast between the joylessness of the son who would not forgive and the rejoicing of the father who forgave.

In this story Jesus provides us with two models: a model of forgiveness, with its resultant joy, and a model of unforgiveness, accompanied by self-pity and withdrawal from "life." Which one we emulate is our decision.

Chapter Six

One Step Further

God didn't stop when He provided the way to settle our original debt. As wonderful as that way was, it didn't provide for any future debts we would incur. God knew that even after we became Christians, we would still sin. To keep us from running up another huge debt, God had another plan.

"If we claim to be without sin, we deceive ourselves and the truth is not in us. If we confess our sins, he is faithful and just and will forgive us our sins and purify us from all unrighteousness. If we claim we have not sinned, we make him out to be a liar and his word has no place in our lives" (1 John 1:8-10).

Rather than having to carry the burden of new sin, we have a way out, if we will accept God's way of doing it. His way is for us to confess our sin to Him. When we do, He forgives us again. In addition, He purifies us. If we choose not to follow God's way, we start accumulating a debt again.

God even makes it easy for us. He takes care of any temptation we might have to deny our sin. Laying it right on the line, He says that if we claim we have not sinned, we are, in effect, calling Him a liar. Confession of the sin is the only way open to us to keep our account free and clear.

When we do that, something in the atonement stretches far beyond the past into the present and the future. It pays the debt for even our current sins, and purifies us in the process.

James adds yet another element to confession. He says, *"Is any one of you sick? He should call the elders of the church to pray over him and anoint him with oil in the name of the Lord. And the prayer offered in faith will make the sick person well; the Lord will raise him up. If he has sinned, he will be forgiven. Therefore, confess your sins to each other and pray for each other so that you may be healed. The prayer of a righteous man is powerful and effective" (Jas. 5:14-16).*

James thrusts so many different ideas at us in these few lines that we need to separate them. Talking in the context of healing, he says: When the elders of the church pray for and anoint the sick person with oil in the name of the Lord, that person will be healed. Then he goes on to say, *"If he has sinned, he will be forgiven,"* the implication being that if the person's illness is caused by sin and he will confess that sin, he will be made well.

Finally, he adds a very important comment. *"Therefore..."* Therefore, what? Therefore, if you are sick, it could be the result of sin in your life, so confess your sins to a fellow Christian and pray for each other—in order to be healed.

We may very well wonder why our sins can't be entirely a matter between God and ourself. Why do James and John add this extra element of confession?

Confessing our sins to another person is one way of curtailing our pride. Most of us have a subconscious fear that we will be exposed as not being such good Christians as we appear to be. Perhaps this is at least part of the reason we are told to confess our sins to one another.

Also, when we involve someone else, it shows we mean business about getting our account with God settled. Then in our times of doubt, we have the additional assurance that we really have been forgiven. Another person's hearing our sins and helping us confess them to God is our witness that the job has truly been accomplished. Finally, we have the extra bonus of another person's prayers added to our own. There is additional strength in corporate prayer.

Perhaps James was also thinking of our very human nature which causes us to commit the same sins over and over again. Perhaps he wisely thought that confessing our sins to at least one other person might act as a deterrent to future sin.

God has provided the complete means by which we can keep our account up to date. But there is a small "service charge." We in turn must continually forgive anyone who sins against us.

Remember the ending to Jesus' story? He told His listeners, *"This is how my heavenly Father will treat each of you unless you forgive your brother from your heart"* (Matt. 18:35).

He repeats this same idea in another passage of scripture: *"For if you forgive men when they sin against you, your heavenly Father will also forgive you. But if you do not forgive men their sins, your*

Father will not forgive your sins" (Matt. 6:14,15).

In order to keep the channel of grace open between God and us, we must forgive others on a continuing basis.

I remember the first time God made me conscious of exactly what I was praying each time I repeated that portion of the Lord's prayer: *"Forgive us our debts, as we also have forgiven our debtors" (Matt. 6:12).*

Don't we all sometimes wish that that line had been omitted? There are occasions when we know we can't sincerely pray that sentence. It isn't what we want. We want God to forgive us, whether or not we are willing to forgive the person who has offended us. But that's not the way it works.

If we will not forgive, what then? What happens to us as our debt to God becomes larger and larger? An old classic, *The Portrait of Dorian Grey,* illustrates this idea extremely well.

In this movie, the chief character, for some reason, never ages or changes externally. However, hidden in his room is a portrait of himself which continually shows the results of the evilness within him. While the man's external features remain handsome, the portrait reveals the increasing hideous condition of his unrepentant soul.

Scripture tells us that when we continue to refuse God's grace, in time our consciences become seared. We become hardened to God's voice. That is the high price paid by those who do not seek God's way of restoration.

God has placed a very high value on forgiveness. Paul, too, emphasized its importance in our Christian walk. Counseling believers, he said, *"Be kind and compassionate to one another, forgiving each other, just as in Christ, God forgave you" (Eph. 4:32).*

The process of forgiveness is ongoing. In order to keep our account clear, we must not only confess our sins to God and ask His forgiveness, but we must continue to forgive others as well.

Chapter Seven

God Doesn't Understand
(Oh, Yes He Does)

Perhaps you're still unconvinced of the necessity of forgiving. Perhaps you even think that God doesn't understand how hard life is. How can He possibly know what He's asking of us?

In our desire to justify our lack of forgiveness, we sometimes forget the time in history when God became man. The Bible tells us:

"For we do not have a High Priest Who is unable to understand and sympathize and have a fellow feeling with our weaknesses and infirmities and liability to the assaults of temptation, but One Who has been tempted in every respect as we are, yet without sinning (Heb. 4:15 TAB).

So it is evident that it was essential that He be made like His brethren in every respect, in order that He might become a merciful (sympathetic) and faithful High Priest in the things related to God, to make atonement and propitiation for the people's sins. For because He Himself (in His humanity) has suffered in being tempted (tested and tried), He is able (immediately) to run to the cry of (assist, relieve) those who are being tempted (tested and tried) and who therefore are being exposed to suffering" (Heb. 2:17,18 TAB).

In simple language, God can require forgiveness of us because He has been there!

These passages made very little impression on me until one day the Holy Spirit began enlivening them and shedding light on an aspect of Jesus' nature I'd never fully considered before.

Previously, I'd seen Jesus as God, rather than man. As God, He'd had resources unavailable to us, so how could He possibly understand what human beings went through? Or so I'd thought. I

25

couldn't have been more wrong. These verses plainly show that we have a God who knows what it is to suffer as we do.

The forgiveness we're called on to give isn't the demand of a righteous God sitting far off in splendor, high above the cares and hurts of people. Rather it is an invitation from a Savior who's actually experienced every pain and sorrow we will ever know, and more. Because of His experiences on earth, there is not an experience we can have with which Jesus doesn't sympathize. Better still, He empathizes with us.

"This High Priest of ours understands our weaknesses since He had the same temptations we do..." (Heb. 4:15 TLB).

With Jesus, it's utterly impossible to say, "But, Lord, you don't understand." He understands only too well.

Do you feel rejected?

No one understands rejection better than Jesus. John 1:11 tells us, *"He came to that which belonged to Him—to His own (domain, creation, things, world)—and they who were His own did not receive Him and did not welcome Him" (John 1:11 TAB).*

From the time of His birth, Jesus was rejected. There was no room for Him at the inn. Later, in an attempt to kill Him, Herod ordered the slaughter of all male babies two years and younger in Bethlehem. During Jesus' earthly ministry, there were constant plots to kill Him. In addition, He was rejected by most of the religious leaders of His day, and even His best friends had trouble understanding Him. Oh, yes, Jesus understands rejection very well.

Are others critical of you?

Jesus is well acquainted with criticism. From the beginning to the end of His ministry, He was criticized by the Jewish leaders.

In John 5:9,10, Jesus is called the Sabbath-breaker because He healed the man beside the Bethesda pool on the Sabbath. The criticism was repeated on another Sabbath when He and His disciples broke off the heads of wheat and ate the grain, a practice which was considered harvesting by the religious authorities of His time.

In Luke 5:30, we see the Pharisees and teachers of the Law complaining about Jesus' eating with *"notorious sinners,"* as do they in Luke 15:1,2. The religious leaders also criticized Him because He did not go through a certain washing ritual (Mark 7:5).

Have your friends deserted you?

At one time or another all of Jesus' disciples deserted Him (Mark 14:50). In addition, Judas betrayed Him.

We're all familiar with how even Peter denied knowing Jesus shortly after His arrest.

Are disobedient children causing you heartache?

One day when I was complaining about the fact that my children were disobedient, God good-naturedly reminded me that He, too, had a few disobedient children.

Are you looked down upon?

The Bible records that Jesus accepted an invitation to dinner at the home of a Pharisee, who then tried to humiliate Him by doing none of the customary acts usually performed by a good host. Jesus had to remind him, *"When I entered your home, you didn't bother to offer me water to wash the dust from my feet... You refused me the customary kiss of greeting... You neglected the usual courtesy of olive oil to anoint my head..." (Luke 7:44,45).*

Jesus was constantly looked down upon by the religious elite of His time, who called Him a *"glutton and a drunkard" (Luke 7:34).*

Do people think you're crazy?

The crowd listening to Jesus at the Tabernacle ceremonies accused Him of being crazy when He said they were trying to kill Him (John 7:20).

Even Jesus' friends suspected Him of being insane. When He returned to the house where He was staying, the crowds began to gather again and soon the house was so full of visitors He couldn't find time to eat. When His friends heard what was happening, they came to take Him home with them. *"'He's out of his mind,' they said" (Mark 3:21).*

Are you scoffed at and ridiculed?

So was Jesus.

When He came to heal Jairus' daughter, He found the home *"filled with mourning people, but he said, 'Stop the weeping! She isn't dead; she is only asleep.'" (Luke 8:52).* This brought scoffing and laughter *"for they all knew she was dead."*

Even His relatives mocked Him. *"'Go where more people can see your miracles!' they scoffed. 'You can't be famous when you hide like this! If you're so great, prove it to the world!' For even his brothers didn't believe in him" (John 7:3-5).*

Has someone proved ungrateful?

Of the ten lepers healed, only one came back to thank Jesus (Luke 17:11-19).

Are you angry because you are unmarried?

Jesus lived His life on earth as a celibate, as a single. He was a step-child. In the judgment of everyone who knew Him, He was a failure.

No, my friend, Jesus' life on earth proves that God understands our problems, our trials, our temptations only too well. It is our turn now to understand Jesus—and His ability to forgive.

Chapter Eight
Coping with Anger

Few of us deliberately set out to be unforgiving. Then what is the tortuous path we take to arrive at this harmful situation?

To answer that question, we need to look at unforgiveness under a strong light. Exactly what is it? Surprisingly enough, unforgiveness is not, as many think, an emotion, although it is always preceded and accompanied by strong emotions. Rather, it is an attitude born out of our nourishing and caring for the emotions of anger and resentment.

The Bible recognizes that there are times when we will become angry. It cautions us to quickly repent of that anger and come to terms with the person or situation that caused it. However, if we refuse, allowing that same anger to germinate and develop into resentment, we are moving into troubled waters. Resentments held onto over a period of time naturally grow into bitterness and once bitterness develops, we have entered into the turbulent arena of unforgiveness.

Cain serves as a ready model to show us the destructiveness of following such a course.

The two sons of Adam and Eve were very different. They even chose different occupations: Abel was a shepherd, while his older brother, Cain, was an orchard man. At harvest time Cain brought the Lord a gift of his produce, while Abel brought the fatty cuts of meat from his best lambs. Although both sons knew that an acceptable offering must involve the shedding of blood, nevertheless, Cain insisted upon bringing his own kind of offering.

The Bible tells us, *"And the Lord accepted Abel's offering, but not Cain's. This made Cain both dejected and very angry, and his face grew dark with fury.*

"'Why are you so angry?' the Lord asked him. 'Why is your face so dark with rage? It can be bright with joy if you will do what you should!'" (Gen. 4:4-7 TLB).

Although the Lord offered Cain another chance, Cain stubbornly brooded over God's *unfairness.* In time, the area of his bitterness extended to include his brother Abel, whose offering God had accepted.

The more Cain brooded, the more he hated Abel. Finally the day came when, on some pretext, he lured Abel out into the fields. Once there, Cain attacked and killed him.

Let's trace Cain's anger from beginning to end. We don't have to read between the lines to recognize that there must have been rebellion in Cain's heart before this incident took place; otherwise, he would have brought an offering acceptable to the Lord. Certainly, God had made his wishes known to the brothers; otherwise, how would they have known to make any kind of sacrifice? We can safely assume that Cain knew beforehand what he was supposed to do and that he rejected the idea for one of his own.

When God did not accept Cain's offering, instead of repenting, Cain took offense. Still, the Lord offered him joy and another chance if he would only do what he was supposed to do. Again, Cain refused the opportunity to repent and be restored to God. Now, as he began to nourish and care for his grievance against God, another factor was added. Cain was no longer angry with God alone; he was also angry with his brother who had chosen God's way. In his mind, he could not "forgive" Abel for being acceptable to God, and so, when his anger had been allowed to fully mature, he murdered Abel.

The secret to avoiding unforgiveness (an attitude) is to establish control over our strong, negative emotions before they have the time and opportunity to harden into attitudes.

The Bible gives us many warnings against anger. The meaning is not always too clear at first glance because translators have taken three different Greek words with four different meanings and translated them into our one English word, *anger* or *angry.*

"In your anger do not sin" (Eph. 4:26).

"Do not let the sun go down while you are still angry" (Eph. 4:26).

"Anyone who is angry with his brother will be subject to judgment" (Matt. 5:22).

The Greek words involved in these verses are *thumos,* which is a passion, a boiling up and quickly subsiding; and *orge,* an anger which is an abiding and settled habit of mind. To add to the confusion, *orge,* under certain circumstances, can also mean a "righteous passion" or as we would say, "righteous indignation." In this case, *orge* is the attitude we should have toward sin, not people.

The scriptures quoted above could more understandably be translated:

"Be *righteously indignant* and sin not."

"Do not let the sun go down on your *boiling-up-and-quickly subsiding* anger."

"Whoever is angry with a *settled and abiding habit of mind* with his brother is in danger of judgment."

A master of disguise, anger in our civilized society is not always easy to detect in all of its forms.

Someone slights us; we don't feel consciously angry; instead we feel "hurt."

A person we love lets us know he no longer returns our love. We burst out crying, feeling a stabbing kind of pain. Yet if we were to carefully unwrap the outer layers of this pain, we would find anger at its core.

Anger can also disguise itself as indifference. The more "civilized" we are, the more unacceptable we find our raw emotions, and the more we are inclined to hide our true feelings, even from ourself. Someone offends us. We don't become overtly angry—in fact, we don't experience the emotion of anger at all. What we do feel is a cold indifference for the other person. We refuse to have anything to do with her.

Sometimes our anger will even appear as sorrow. Many widows vascillate between feelings of grief, hopelessness, and anger. When their anger is allowed expression, they may find themselves almost hating their dead husbands at times. "How could he leave me alone?" they demand irrationally. "He knew I couldn't live alone. He should have let me die first."

Many doctors now recognize that anger is a part of normal grief when we lose someone we love. They know that if the person is ever to recover, she must face the fact of her anger over the "desertion" and come to terms with it. Part of that working through is to forgive the deceased husband for abandoning her.

Anger is our human response to anyone or anything that hurts us. We experience that boiling up and quickly subsiding kind of anger that happens almost spontaneously. A car cuts us off in traffic, someone sneaks in ahead of us in the supermarket line, we trip over one of the kid's toys, our husband forgets to mail an important letter. Whether we should or not, we become temporarily angry. The important thing, however, is not to retain that anger.

That is why we are cautioned not to let "the sun go down on" it.

When we have given way to this kind of anger, we must treat it as any sin. We must confess it to God and, if need be, make amends to anyone else involved. Should we find ourself retaining the anger even after confession, we may need to discuss the situation that caused it with anyone else involved and reach a better understanding with them. Admitting our anger may be a blow to our pride, but we need to reach the point where our relationships with others are too important to endanger with our bad temper.

"Be righteously angry and sin not."

It is extremely difficult for us as human beings to hate the sin without hating the sinner and wishing him harm. Yet, if we are ever to be *righteously* angry, we must carefuly follow this rule, lest our anger become sin.

Finally, in dealing with that *abiding and settled habit of mind* type of anger, we must be very careful and, if necessary, get counseling. This, in particular is the kind of anger Jesus warns against. It is this kind of anger that has been responsible for much of the bloodshed on earth. It is this kind of anger that breeds unforgiveness.

Chapter Nine
How We Forgive

"*Then Peter came to Jesus and asked, 'Lord how many times shall I forgive my brother when he sins against me? Up to seven times?'*

"*Jesus answered, 'I tell you, not seven times, but seventy-seven times'*" *(Matt. 18:21,22).*

Most of us know we are supposed to forgive; few of us want to hang on to our resentments; no one deliberately sets out to become bitter. But wanting to forgive and knowing how to are two different things. Just exactly how do we forgive?

Forgiveness is rarely easy. Certainly, it is not some words glibly spoken and having no substance. Forgiveness is frequently costly; look at what it cost God—the death of His Son; look at what it cost Jesus—His life.

If we are to be like our Lord, forgiveness will cost us something, too, and sometimes the price is high.

What is this price? First of all, to forgive means giving up our right to be hurt and to return hurt. This is not to say that we won't be hurt. We will be, but we must give up the *right* to be hurt, the right to feel pain and anger over what someone else does to us. The natural man feels he has a right to avenge himself. Or at least to the more civilized approach: "You hurt me; I wouldn't think of retaliating; I'll even forgive you, but I just don't want to have anything more to do with you."

That is not the Lord's way.

Listen to what Jesus says,

"*You have heard that it was said, 'Eye for eye, and tooth for tooth.' But I tell you, 'Do not resist an evil person. If someone strikes you on the right cheek, turn to him the other also. And if someone wants to sue you and take your tunic, let him have your cloak as well. If someone forces you to go one mile, go with him two miles. Give to the one who asks you, and do not turn away from the one who wants to borrow from you.*

"You have heard that it was said, 'Love your neighbor and hate your enemy.' But I tell you: 'Love your enemies and pray for those who persecute you, that you may be sons of your Father in heaven'" (Matt. 5:38-45).

Jesus will not support our demands for our "rights." Remember the man who called to Jesus, *"Teacher, tell my brother to divide the inheritance with me.' Jesus' response was, 'Man, who appointed me a judge or an arbiter between you?'" (Luke 12:13,14).*

Paul reflected this same attitude when, in criticizing the Corinthian church for not settling their disputes among themselves, but taking them to court, asked, *"Why not rather be wronged? Why not rather be cheated?" (1 Cor. 6:7).*

Janie learned the difficulty of doing this recently. Long before her grown son, Jim, ever became a Christian, she had ordered an expensive Bible for him and had his name engraved on it. The Bible remained at the book store, awaiting the day Jim would come to the Lord. This past year it happened. Jim did accept Jesus and Janie was delighted. However, the next day the owner of the book store called to tell her that Jim's wife, who knew all about Janie's would-be gift, had come into the store that day and also ordered a Bible for Jim. What should she do?

Knowing what she should do did not make the act any less painful for Janie. "Let Miriam give him the Bible," she told her friend. "It's probably more important that it come from her than from me."

The words were easier to say than to mean with her whole heart. "It was hard to forgive Miriam," Janie admitted. "She knew how many years I had wanted to give Jim a Bible. But I also was not going to allow my son to start out his Christian walk with bad feelings between Miriam and me."

Forgiving also means that we are willing to be vulnerable. Whenever we forgive someone, we assume the risk that that person may hurt us again.

Ed and Harriet have remained vulnerable through some extremely traumatic experiences with their daughter, Sherry. When she was seventeen, Sherry ran away from home, ending up in a "hippie" commune where she met a man named Ward. A short time later, she and Ward left the commune to live together. A year later, they showed up at her parents' home, confessed they were tired of their lifestyle and wanted to go "straight." Ed and Harriet gave them a large wedding, which was held in their garden on a lovely summer day.

Less than a year later, Sherry and Ward separated and Sherry moved in and out of a series of relationships with different men, eventually returning to Ward who had never stopped loving her.

Ed and Harriet forgave her once again and prayed that Sherry, who was now willing to go to church, had finally seen the light. However, it was not to be. Sherry now became desperate to have a child. After several miscarriages, she became despondent and moved out of her home to try the "swinging single" lifestyle once more.

This time her escapade led her into the hard drug scene, a stolen credit card and forged checks. Eventually caught, she was convicted and given a suspended sentence on condition that she repay the stolen money which she'd already spent.

When she showed up at her parents' doorstep, once more repentant, they found forgiving her again to be no simple matter.

"Sherry has violated every principle we believe in," Harriet told her pastor. "We had such high hopes for our daughter, but at this point I'd like to take my losses and get out of the whole picture. I don't wish her any harm, but I really wish she'd just disappear out of our lives."

But Sherry was not going to simply disappear, and neither was Harriet and Ed's anger. The couple sadly realized that no matter who was at fault, the anger was entirely their problem. Unless they wanted to continue to live with the discomfort and anger against Sherry for perhaps the rest of their lives, they were going to have to truly forgive their daughter once and for all.

They don't pretend to have reached the goal of total forgiveness, but they have made great strides in that direction. How?

"By giving up a lot of our expectations for Sherry," Harriet explained, "but most of all by being willing to be hurt again. In the back of my mind I had this fantasy that someday Sherry would return home and say, 'You've always been right, Mom and Daddy. Please forgive me. I'm going to do things your way now.'

"I just gave it up. I also gave up the ideal of not ever being hurt by her again. Sherry probably will hurt us again. That's okay. Our security is in God. We'll go on praying for her and be around to pick up the pieces if it ever gets to that point again."

Forgiveness also means having sufficient faith in the future to let go of the past. We are tied to anything we resent or hate. The person who angers us chains us to the past with unbreakable links. Such a person absorbs our thinking, becomes a constant cellmate. The only way we can be free of those we resent is to loose them—free them once and for all by forgiving them. Like Paul, we must *"forget those things behind us."*

We can forgive when we recognize that forgiveness is not a sign of weakness, but a stance of strength.

The world believes that forgiving someone indicates weakness. "Give an inch and they'll take a mile," is the attitude expressed by man. Allowing someone to get away "with something" doesn't make sense to the non-Christian.

Yet, it was not weakness that caused Jesus to deliver Himself to that cruel mob who demanded His death. It was not weakness that kept him on the cross when He could have called for a legion of angels; neither was it weakness that made Him cry out to His Father, *"Father, forgive them."*

Rather, forgiveness is the stance of strength. For us who are being conformed to the image of our Lord, it is saying, "In Jesus, I am strong, so strong that I can handle any hurt—any injustice you can do to me—and never stop loving you, never stop forgiving you."

It is seeing through the eyes of Joseph whose own brothers had sold him into slavery. Even though the hurt has been deliberate we can say with Joseph, *"You intended to harm me, but God intended it for good to accomplish what is now being done..."* (Gen. 50:20).

Not only is forgiveness the stance of strength; there is also a strength that flows out of forgiveness.

Here is Marion's story:

"My father and mother divorced when I was eight years old. He married the lady I was named after, and they had a financially comfortable life with her daughter and family. My mother, sister, and I moved thousands of miles away and with little income, had to scrimp and scrape. Dad only wrote once a year, sending Christmas gifts inappropriate for my age level at the time and only indicating to me that he had not chosen them with much care. He would say, 'I love you,' but I didn't believe that for a minute.

"Eighteen years later, at the time of the birth of my third son, Dad decided he wanted to become an active part of my life. At the time I made a choice with my will to allow my sons the joy of knowing their grandfather, but it was only after I had made the Lord, *lord* of my life some nine years later that I began to see the need to forgive my father. All the bitterness, hatred, anger, disappointment, etc. surfaced as the Lord shone His healing love in those dark places. I finally came to a place where I wanted a truly right relationship with my dad.

"The Lord arranged for me to fly to California where my father was living and a time of forgiveness and cleansing was experienced by both of us. We melted into each other's arms and wept like babies, filled with the wonder of how God could eradicate in a second of time all the pain of the past thirty years.

"As a direct result of his seeing Jesus in me, that very next day my dad renewed his long forgotten commitment to God. He was baptized in the Holy Spirit and received a healing of deafness with the result that he discarded a $500 hearing aid he no longer needed. We sang in tongues all the way on that half-hour drive home the next day!"

When we are willing to relinquish our rights, to be vulnerable, to put the past behind us, to take the position of strength, rather than weakness, then God is free to work that forgiveness through. Nowhere has His willingness to do this been illustrated more beautifully, than in the life of Corrie ten Boom.

"It was at a church service in Munich that I saw him, the former S.S. man who had stood guard at the shower room door in the processing center at Ravensbruck. He was the first of our actual jailers that I had seen since that time. And suddenly it was all there—the roomful of mocking men, the heaps of clothing, Betsie's pain-blanched face.

"He came up to me as the church was emptying, beaming and bowing. 'How grateful I am for your message, Fraulein,' he said. 'To think that, as you say, He has washed my sins away!'"

"His hand was thrust out to shake mine. And I, who had preached so often to the people in Bloemendaal the need to forgive, kept my hand at my side.

"Even as the angry, vengeful thoughts boiled through me, I saw the sin of them. Jesus Christ had died for this man; was I going to ask for more? 'Lord, Jesus,' I prayed, 'forgive me and help me to forgive him.'

"I tried to smile. I struggled to raise my hand. I could not. I felt nothing, not the slightest spark of warmth or charity. And so again I breathed a silent prayer. 'Jesus, I cannot forgive him. Give me Your forgiveness.'

"As I took his hand the most incredible thing happened. From my shoulder along my arm and through my hand a current seemed to pass from me to him, while into my heart sprang a love for this stranger that almost overwhelmed me.'"*

When we are truly willing to forgive—if necessary, God will even provide the forgiveness. But we must be willing. When we are, God not only forgives us, but He is free to release His miraculous love through us in ways He can't under other circumstances.

*Corrie Ten Boom, *The Hiding Place* (Chosen Books)

In this present great move of God, God will supernaturally touch the hearts of many. Others will not believe until they see the principles of the Kingdom in action. One of the chief ways these principles will be demonstrated will be by our giving flesh to them—by our forgiveness of one another.

Let us begin to forgive!